COST OF LIVING.

Until 1971, the British pound (£) was divided into 20 shillings (s.), and the shilling into 12 pennies (d.). As a child working in a cotton mill in 1842, you'd be likely to earn about 3s. a week. If you're paying 2s. a week for rent, this leaves you just 1s. to spend. How would you spend your shilling?

Large loaf of bread: 8d.
Pint of milk: 1d.
1 lb* oatmeal: 2d.
5 lb potatoes: 2d.
1 lb tea: 4s. 0d.
1 lb sugar: 8d.

1 lb butter: 1s. 0d.
12 eggs: 8d.
1 lb bacon: 8d.
1 lb soap: 6d.
1 lb candles: 6d.
Bag of coal: 1s. 6d.

*"lb" stands for one pound weight.

See page 13 for more information on the value of money then and now.

Author:

John Malam studied ancient history and archaeology at the University of Birmingham, England. He then worked as an archaeologist at the Ironbridge Gorge Museum in Shropshire. He is now an author, specializing in nonfiction books for children. He lives in Cheshire with his wife and their two young children. Website: www.johnmalam.co.uk

Artist:

David Antram was born in Brighton, England, in 1958. He studied at Eastbourne College of Art and then worked in advertising for fifteen years before becoming a full-time artist. He has illustrated many children's nonfiction books.

Series creator:

David Salariya was born in Dundee, Scotland. He has illustrated a wide range of books and has created and designed many new series for publishers in the UK and overseas. In 1989 he established The Salariya Book Company. He lives in Brighton with his wife, illustrator Shirley Willis, and their son Jonathan.

Editor: **Stephen Haynes**

Editorial Assistant: **Mark Williams**

© The Salariya Book Company Ltd MMVII
No part of this publication may be reproduced in whole or in part, or stored in a retrieval system, or transmitted in any form or by any means, electronic, mechanical, photocopying, recording, or otherwise, without written permission of the publisher. For information regarding permission, write to Scholastic Inc., 557 Broadway, New York, NY 10012.

Published in Great Britain in 2007 by
The Salariya Book Company Ltd
25 Marlborough Place, Brighton BN1 1UB

ISBN-13: 978-0-531-18747-0 (lib. bdg.)   978-0-531-13928-8 (pbk.)
ISBN-10: 0-531-18747-0 (lib. bdg.)   0-531-13928-X (pbk.)

All rights reserved.
Published in 2008 in the United States
by Franklin Watts
An imprint of Scholastic Inc.
Published simultaneously in Canada.

A CIP catalog record for this book is available
from the Library of Congress.

Printed and bound in China.
Printed on paper from sustainable sources.

SCHOLASTIC, FRANKLIN WATTS, and associated logos are trademarks and/or registered trademarks of Scholastic Inc.

So this is Manchester...

You Wouldn't Want to Be a Victorian Mill Worker!

A Grueling Job You'd Rather Not Have

Written by
John Malam

Illustrated by
David Antram

Created and designed by
David Salariya

Franklin Watts®
An Imprint of Scholastic Inc.
NEW YORK • TORONTO • LONDON • AUCKLAND • SYDNEY
MEXICO CITY • NEW DELHI • HONG KONG
DANBURY, CONNECTICUT

Contents

Introduction

The year is 1842, and Britain is the workshop of the world. Its factories are churning out more goods than ever before. Towns are getting bigger and busier, and they're being linked together by the rapidly expanding railway network. Nowhere are these changes more obvious than in the county of Lancashire, in the northwest of England. The southern part of the county is the world center of the cotton-making industry, and it seems that every town has lots of noisy, dusty mills and smoke-belching chimneys. Go inside one of these "dark Satanic mills" (as the poet William Blake put it in 1804) and you'll meet workers who are slaves to the machines. And you, my boy, are one of them.

I'm eleven (I think). I'm old enough to do a day's work.

FIELD TO MILL. Cotton is grown in the southern states of the United States, shipped to the port of Liverpool, England, then taken to the mill towns of Lancashire to be made into cloth.

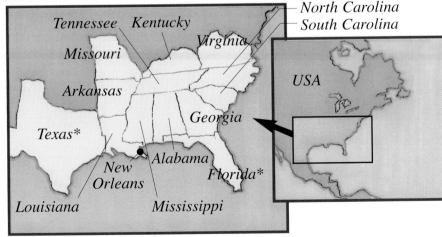

Tennessee Kentucky
Missouri Virginia North Carolina
South Carolina
Arkansas
Georgia
Texas*
Alabama
New Orleans Florida*
Louisiana Mississippi

USA

Great Britain

Lancashire
Preston Blackburn Rochdale
Bolton
Wigan Oldham
Manchester
Liverpool

*Texas and Florida were not separate states until 1845

5

Cotton! The American Connection

The mills of Lancashire are hungry for cotton fiber, which they turn into valuable cotton cloth. But the cotton plant doesn't grow anywhere near Lancashire. It thrives in warm, dry parts of the world, not in Lancashire's cool, damp climate. And so the cotton that these British mills depend on has to come all the way from India, Egypt, and, most of all, the United States.

In the United States, cotton is grown mostly in the southern states of Alabama, Georgia, North Carolina, South Carolina, and Virginia. All across this vast area, which is known as the "Cotton Belt," are plantations where slaves plant, grow, and harvest fields of cotton. Between September and November, a slave picks around 100 pounds of raw cotton every day—and it's this "white gold" that you'll see coming into your mill.

PLANTING
April–May

GROWING
April–November

HARVEST
September–November

GINNING.
A cotton gin breaks open the cotton bolls (seed heads) and separates the valuable cotton fibers from the seeds.

BALING. Ginned cotton is pressed into bales. American bales are taller than a man, and weigh about 400 pounds.

TRANSPORTING. Bales are shipped to the southern port of New Orleans...

...then ships take them to Liverpool, England.

STARS AND STRIPES. This is what the U.S. flag looks like in 1842, with 26 stars on it, one for each state in the Union.

Handy Hint

Pick the cotton before it rains —there will be trouble if it gets wet!

Y'all pick faster now —rain's a-comin'!

Slavery was abolished in the British Empire in 1833, and in the United States in 1865.

7

Your Woeful Workhouse Work

In the workhouse you had to:

CRUSH BONE (used to make fertilizer).

PICK OAKUM. Pick apart rope to make oakum (used to make ships watertight).

CHOP WOOD into pieces for firewood.

BREAK STONE into little bits for use in road repairs.

Fate has dealt you a hard life, and it's not about to get any easier. Your family came to England from Ireland in search of work, and what happened? Your father was killed building one of the new railway lines! With no money to support the family, your mother had no choice but to seek help from the parish. That's how you ended up in a workhouse in London. In return for food and shelter, you have to work hard. And all along you've dreamed of a day like today, when a rich mill owner will come to your rescue. He needs boys like you to work in his mill in Manchester, where life will be better… you hope.

You'll have to learn to understand Lancashire dialect!

Wossupwithi? (What is the matter with you?)

Mother!

8

Will Your New Home Really Be This Good?

Fine clothes, good food, plenty of pocket money... you can only hope!

Handy Hint

Before you leave, ask your friends to tell your mother where you are going. She might come after you, one day.

My poor child!

Manchester! Dirty New Town

SIGN HERE. The mill owner makes you sign an agreement that binds you to work for him until you are 21 years old. You've never been taught to write, so you sign it with your mark.

I t's taken three long, bumpy days to travel the 185 miles by road from London to Manchester, and your dream of a better life has become a nightmare. Fine clothes, good food, pocket money? Forget it! Manchester in 1842 is a boom town, with around 100 cotton mills all squeezed close to its center. Their chimneys rise high into the sky. Gray smoke covers the town like a dirty blanket and blocks out the sunlight. You've moved in with an Irish family that lives in the district called Little Ireland—a rat-infested slum along the banks of the River Medlock. There are 4,000 poor people here, and your landlady and her family live in the cellar of one of the houses. It's gloomy, cold, and very damp, and there are no windows. Welcome to your new home!

Home, Sweet Home?

MANCHESTER. 240,000 people live here. They call it "Cottonopolis" (cotton city) because of its mills.

BED AND BOARD. You'll share a bed with your landlady's grubby children. You'll eat potatoes, bread, porridge, milk, and sometimes eggs and bacon.

Factory Slave! This Is Your Life

Daily Grind

🕐 5:00 a.m.
Get up, get dressed, eat bread, drink milk, make lunch.

🕐 5:15 a.m.
Hear mill bell, walk to work.

🕐 5:30 a.m.
Start work.

🕐 7:30 a.m.
Clean machines.

🕐 12:00 noon
Clean machines, eat lunch.

🕐 7:00 p.m.
Machines stop; clean them, go home.

Every day is the same. Your landlady is too poor to own a clock, so a "bobber" or "knocker-up" wakes you up at daybreak with a loud knock at the cellar door. In no time at all, you're ready for a long day's work at the mill. It's a tall, red brick building at the edge of the River Medlock, and you are one of the 250 people who work there. Nine years ago, in 1833, the government made a law that said children under the age of 9 must not work in the cotton mills. The same law said that children aged 9 to 13 could only work nine hours a day in the mills—but your mill owner gets away with making you work 13½ hours a day! No wonder Lancashire's mill workers feel like slaves.

Thaz a face like a line a wet weshin!
(You have a face like a line of wet washing!) (It means "Stop sulking.")

Who's Who at the Mill

MILL MANAGER.

MILL OWNER. He's the big boss. Nobody argues with him.

He's in charge of all the workers.

OVERLOOKERS are in charge of each work room in the mill.

I am not happy in Manchester . . . hideous mill prisons for children . . . huge factories overhanging the sky . . .

EYEWITNESS. The artist Benjamin Haydon visited Manchester in June 1837, and wrote about it in his diary.

What can you buy with the money you earn at the mill? See page 1.

See page 1.

Handy Hint

Don't run away. If you get caught you'll be fined and your hair will be cut off.

What did you say?

WEEKLY PAY.
Spinner (adult): 25 shillings (£1.25) — though he's only left with about 16 shillings (80p) because he has to pay his piecers
Carder (adult): 9 shillings (45p)
Piecer (child): about 3 shillings (15p), depending on age and experience

FINES.
Opening window: 1 shilling (5p)
Taking a wash: 1 shilling (5p)
Late for work: 1 shilling (5p)
Whistling: 1 shilling (5p)
Leaving gaslight on: 2 shillings (10p)

1842 →	Value in U.S. Dollars Today
5p	$6.83
10p	$13.65
15p	$20.50
45p	$61.50
80p	$109.35
£1.25	$170.90

ENGINEERS AND MECHANICS look after the mill's machinery.

FURNACEMEN shovel coal into the boiler that powers the mill's steam engine. Hot work!

MACHINE OPERATORS. So-called "Lancashire mill lasses"—young women who work the machines.

CHILDREN assist the machine operators, doing boring and often dangerous work.

Cleaning the Cotton

After three weeks at sea, the bales of American cotton reach Liverpool. Some then travel the final 36 miles of their journey along the new railway line to Manchester, but rail travel is expensive, so most bales go by road.

At the mill, the process of turning cotton into thread, or yarn, begins. The bales enter the mixing room. They're ripped open and the raw cotton is pulled out by mixers as young as you. It's stuffed into a scutcher, which is a machine with a big drum. Inside, the cotton is beaten to remove the trash—seeds, leaves, stalks, dirt, and so on. The scutcher cleans the cotton and makes it into a light and fluffy fleece called the "lap." It's noisy, dusty work, and the air is filled with cotton fibers that make you cough and choke. You can hardly breathe!

Children's Work

MIXER. You pull cotton from the bales with your hands and put it into the scutcher.

Clatter!

Clatter!

Clatter!

Making Cotton Yarn: Part 1

The raw cotton is turned into the lap, which is used in the next stage.

1. Wagons bring the bales to the mill.

Handy Hint

Tie a damp cloth around your nose and mouth to stop you from choking on the cotton fibers in the air.

2. The bales are chopped open in the mixing room.

3. The scutching machine makes the lap.

Carding the Cotton and Carrying the Can

DUSTY WORK.

CARDER'S COUGH is caused by breathing in cotton dust.

HOT AND DAMP. The heat and moisture inside the mill are good for the cotton, but the workers end up with fevers and shivers.

From the mixing room you'll carry the rolls of lap into the carding room. You're one of the mill's many child doffers, and it's your job to doff (fetch and carry). The carding machines work like giant combs. They straighten out the twisted and knotted cotton fibers in the lap and turn them into long white ropes, called "slivers." The slivers leave the machines and coil themselves into tall, round boxes called carding canisters, or "cans" for short.

The machines are operated by carders, and you'll be working for one of these wheezing, coughing men. He'll keep you busy, fetching the lap to the machines, loading it onto them, and replacing the full cans with empty ones. In fact, the carder will have you "carrying the can" all day long!

CARDING BY HAND. Before the carding machine was invented in 1748, cotton had to be carded by hand.

TANGLED TO STRAIGHT. Carding straightens out the tangled mass of cotton fibers.

Making Cotton Yarn: Part 2

The doffer—that's you— loads the carding machine with a roll of lap. It cards the lap to make a sliver of cotton. The cotton sliver is used in the next stage.

Children's Work

DOFFER. You don't need to be a genius for this job, but you do need to pay attention, stay awake, and work fast.

Handy Hint

Be quick! Don't run out of empty cans, or the cotton slivers will spill onto the floor.

Clatter! Clatter!

I didn't mean to drop it!

Cack-'anded clotyead!
(Clumsy cloth-head!)

4. The lap is loaded onto the carding machine.

5. Slivers of carded cotton fall into carding cans.

6. Full cans are switched for empty ones.

17

Spinning the Cotton

The spinning room is the heart of the mill. Machines called mules, that are up to 200 feet long, roll backward and forward over the floor. They take yarn that's already been given a loose twist on a drawing frame (this is called "roving yarn"), and twist it tighter. They also stretch it to even out any rough parts. Each mule has up to 1,200 spindles that whiz round 150 times a second. As they spin, they wind the yarn onto wooden bobbins at the incredible rate of 7 miles every minute.

It's hot inside the spinning room, and the floor is slippery from the oil that drips from the mules. As these massive machines clatter across the floor, children work beneath them, tying the ends of broken yarn together and sweeping up the fluff. This is very dangerous work.

You on t'flooer! Wilta wark fasser!
(You on the floor! Will you work faster?)

Making Cotton Yarn: Part 3

Slivers pulled from the cans are drawn into a thread which has a loose twist in it (roving yarn). It's given a tighter twist by the mules, and wound onto bobbins.

7. The drawing frame turns slivers into roving yarn.

8. Spinning mules twist the yarn more tightly.

18

Children! Children!

Yes, sir. I'll try, sir.

Handy Hint

Don't wear clogs in the spinning room. You'll get a better grip on the oily floor if you work barefoot.

Children's Work

LITTLE PIECER. Threads break all the time—little children piece (join) them together.

BIG PIECER. An older boy who's learning to be a spinner.

SCAVENGER. Works under the spinning mules, brushing fluff and dirt off the floor.

LAP JOINER. Joins pieces of sliver together at the drawing frame by rolling them in his hands.

There are many different kinds of bobbins.

9. Bobbins hold the spun yarn.

19

Weaving Yarn into Cloth

The weaving shed is where the yarn is woven into long lengths of cloth. It's packed with hundreds of power looms, and is the noisiest room in the whole mill. The noise comes from the nonstop rising and falling of the frames that carry the yarn on the looms, and from the picking-sticks. The sticks jerk backward and forward, batting a shuttle across the warp threads—the threads that run the length of the cloth. The shuttle carries the weft thread, which runs the width of the cloth. It travels back and forth 200 times a minute, passing the weft over and under the warp threads. One weaver looks after several looms at a time, with only a child to help him. Get weaving!

Power looms (below) stand close together in long rows.

Wesh yer yeroles!
(Wash your earholes!)

Clatter!

Rumble!

Click!

Pardon, sir?
Can't hear you, sir.

20

Children's Work

TENTER. You help the weaver by keeping an eye on his looms and pointing out any problems, such as broken threads.

Handy Hint

No one can hear you in here, so use "lip language." Exaggerate words with your lips, and you'll "speak" without making a sound!

Finishing the Cloth

BLEACHING AND DYEING.
Woven cloth is soaked in bleach to make it perfectly white. Then it's ready to be dyed a color.

PRINTING.
Printing machines print patterns onto long lengths of woven cloth, using many different colors.

Smack!

nir!

KISS THE SHUTTLE.
Yarn has to be threaded through the shuttle. The easiest way to do it is to "kiss" the shuttle. Suck hard, and the thread comes through the hole.

Look Out! Dangers of the Mill

If the overseers don't get you, the work will:

CUT FINGERS. Watch out for the sharp metal pins on the carding machines — they'll prick your fingers.

herever you are in the mill, you are close to life-threatening danger. In the mixing room your hands will be red and raw from tugging at the bales of cotton, and in the carding room you'll cough and splutter like an old man, not to mention the cuts you'll get from the prickly pins on the carding machines. The mules in the spinning room will run you down, and no one will hear you scream in the weaving shed.

And if you're tempted to sneak a minute or two of rest, don't. An overseer will find your hiding place, and then you'll feel his stick or strap on your backside.

The mill is so hot and humid that when you go outside your body finds it difficult to get used to the sudden change in temperature. It's a tough life.

CRUSHED. If you're working under a mule, roll away from its wheels — they're heavy enough to kill you.

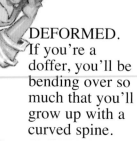

DEFORMED. If you're a doffer, you'll be bending over so much that you'll grow up with a curved spine.

EAR BASHING. A mill is one of the noisiest places you can imagine — you're very likely to go deaf.

BAD CHEST. All that cotton dust in the air is bad for your lungs — you can expect lung disease and a throaty cough.

Yer munna do it, yer jessy! (You must not do it, you sissy!)

ITCHY EYES. Cotton fibers in the air get into your eyes, making them swollen, sore, and very itchy.

TUBERCULOSIS. You'll catch this painful coughing disease from weavers, who leave germs on the shuttles they kiss.

SCALPED. Long hair and machines don't mix. It's so easy to be dragged into one by your hair.

Fire! Trouble at T'Mill

Accidents happen—and not just to the mill's unfortunate workers. The very worst type of accident is a boiler explosion that ignites the cotton fibers in the air. These tiny, invisible specks are everywhere, and they cause far more than ticklish coughs and itches. Once they're alight, they spread fire from room to room in a flash, and before you know it the whole mill is a raging inferno.

Nothing can save the mill. The fire brigade does its best to put the flames out by squirting water pumped up from the river. But it's too late, and the walls come tumbling down.

NOT FIREPROOF! The mill you worked in was an old one. If it had been a so-called fireproof mill with an iron frame, the damage would not have been so bad.

FIRE SPREADS. It doesn't take much for the fire to spread to nearby mills, and from them it moves to the houses in Little Ireland. Your lodgings catch fire, leaving you homeless.

That's where I work!

Nay more, lad! Tis jiggered! (No longer, boy! It's wrecked!)

25

Hard Times! No Work, No Home

Just when you thought it couldn't get any worse, it has. You've lost your job because the mill has burned down, and you have nowhere to live because your cellar has gone up in smoke. You're forced onto the streets to beg for your living. On top of all that, there's trouble in Lancashire's mill towns. When mill owners try to reduce workers' pay, the mill workers talk of stopping work.

The big day comes on August 8, 1842, when the mill workers call a strike. Men, women, and children stop work and walk out of the mills.

Spare a penny, governor?

General Strike, 1842

All out, lads!

STOP WORK! There's a call for a "Grand National Turn-Out"—for workers to walk out of their mills and go on strike.

BLAN

PETITION. More than three million people sign a petition asking the government to help the working poor.

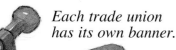

Each trade union has its own banner.

Oi! Mind mi noddle! (Excuse me! Mind my head!)

The strike leaders demand better pay and reduced hours of work, and a petition is sent to the government. But it all goes horribly wrong. Troops shoot at the strikers, the leaders are arrested, and the strike fizzles out in September. Workers drift back to their jobs, and work as they did before. What else can they do?

Handy Hint

Don't despair! There might be work at other mills, so go along and ask.

Get back to work, you idle lot!

BANG!

POP!

PARLIAMENT. More than fifty men carry the petition into parliament. When the government rejects it, riots break out.

"PLUG PLOT." Workers pull plugs from boilers to stop the machinery.

27

Things Can Only Get Better...

Once the strike is over, life returns to normal for you. The mills operate as they did before, and you find work piecing, doffing, and scavenging in another mill. But then two years later, in 1844, your mill is visited by a factory inspector. He writes a long report for the government about the children who work in mills and factories. Because of the report, the government makes a new law that says children aged 8 to 13 must work fewer hours, and they must go to school! In Lancashire's mills, children like you become "half timers"—and at last life really does start to get better.

SCHOOL: Half the day, Monday through Saturday

Now, what comes next?

How old are you, boy?

FACTORY INSPECTOR. The government inspectors ask the mill children lots of questions about their work.

POLITICIANS. The country's leaders have made a new law that says how many hours a day children are allowed to work.

Work half a day, school half a day.

MILL: Half the day, Monday through Saturday

Handy Hint
Remember the half-timers' chant:
"No school, no mill;
no mill, no money."

Can't wait to go to school!

This is your day of rest.

DAY OFF: Sunday

My child!

I've missed you, too!

FAMILY REUNITED. Good news! Your workhouse friends told your mother where you were going. As soon as she could leave the workhouse she came to Manchester to find you. Now you'll never be separated from her again.

Glossary

Bale Raw cotton that has been pressed into a large bundle.

Bobber A person who knocks on house doors and windows to wake the occupants; also called a "knocker-up."

Bobbin The wooden tube that finished yarn is wound onto.

Can A tall, round box that holds a sliver of cotton.

Carding Combing cotton fibers to make them straight.

Cholera A deadly disease spread by infected water, which causes diarrhea, sickness, pain, and thirst.

Clogs The everyday shoes of working people in Lancashire: strong leather boots with wooden soles strengthened by iron strips.

Cotton Belt The region of the southern United States where cotton grows.

Doffer A worker who fetches and carries ("doffs") for another person.

Drawing frame A machine that puts the first loose twist into the yarn.

Ginning Separating cotton fibers from the cotton seeds in a gin machine. "Gin" comes from the word "engine."

Half-timer In Lancashire, a child who works part-time at a mill, and goes to school for the rest of the time.

Lap Soft, fleecy cotton fibers after they have been cleaned by the scutcher.

Lip language Exaggerated movements of the lips and face, used to communicate in a noisy place.

Mixer A person who puts raw cotton into the scutcher.

Mule A machine that spins cotton. It does the work of two other machines, and is called a "mule" to show that it's made from both of them—just as a real mule is half-donkey, half-horse.

Oakum Untwisted fibers of old rope, stuffed between the planks of wooden ships to keep them watertight.

Overlooker A person in charge of a room in the mill.

Petition A request signed by a large number of people who want something to be changed.

Piecer A person who pieces (joins) broken threads together.

Power loom A machine for weaving yarn into cloth.

Roving Loosely twisted yarn made by the drawing frame.

Scavenger A person who sweeps the floor under the spinning mules.

Scutcher A machine that cleans the trash from raw cotton.

Shuttle A wooden container that carries the weft thread across the warp on the loom.

Sliver A rope of cotton made by a carding machine.

Slum A very poor type of house.

Strike When workers stop work in demand for better pay and working conditions.

Tenter A person who helps a weaver.

Trade union An association of workers who get together to demand better pay and conditions.

Trash Seeds, leaves, and stalks mixed up with the cotton fibers.

Troglodyte A cave dweller; also a person who lives in the dark, damp cellar of a house.

Warp The threads that run along the length of the cloth.

Weft The threads that run across the width of the cloth; also called "woof."

Workhouse A place where poor people were given food and housing in return for doing work.

Yarn Cotton that has been spun into a fine thread.

Index